Diamonds

What you need to know
to talk smart about diamonds!

Angelo Tropea

ISBN-13: 978-1986909655

ISBN-10: 1986909654

Diamonds are accepted all over the world as a symbol of commitment and true and eternal love.

Round Brilliant

The most popular diamond shape.

Contents

Introduction

What is the definition of diamond?

A *diamond* is a stone used in jewelry and industrial applications. They are a form of carbon. Natural diamonds are usually clear and colorless, and after they are cut and polished, they are prized as precious gems.

From where does the word diamond come from?

The word, *diamond* comes from the Greek word "adamao" ("I subdue" or "I tame"). *Adámas* (unbreakable) is the adjective form.

What material makes up diamonds?

Diamonds are composed of carbon atoms arranged in what is referred to as a diamond lattice (a regular three-dimensional arrangement of atoms). It is the hardest natural material and twice as hard as silicon nitride and cubic boron nitride (the diamond's closest competitor).

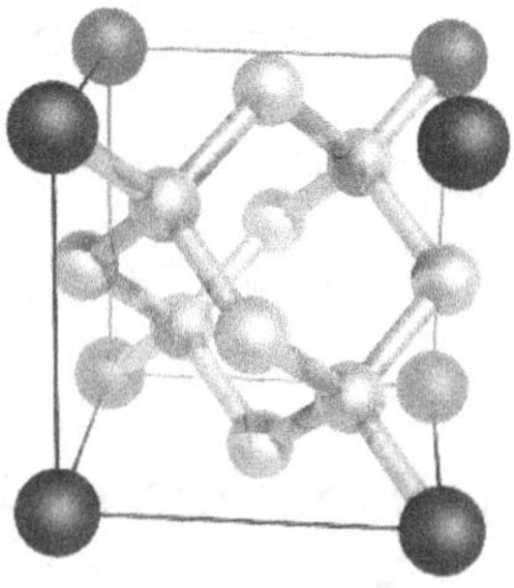

Diamond Lattice

How are diamonds formed?

Diamonds are formed in depths of 87 to 118 miles (140 to 190 kilometers) below the surface of the earth. The high temperature and pressure causes carbon-containing minerals to be squeezed into diamond form. This natural process is <u>not</u> quick. It can take 1 billion to 3.3 billion years! Generally, the longer the growing period, the larger the diamond.

Are there diamonds in space?

Some diamonds may have been brought to earth by meteorites! Scientists also believe that diamonds exist on alien planets and that "diamond rain" forms on Uranus, Neptune, Saturn, and Jupiter (and perhaps other countless alien planets?).
The planet 55 Cancri is hypothesized by some scientists to be made predominantly of diamonds.
Even if we could travel there, its distance from earth (40.12 light years) would make the cost of transporting the diamonds truly "astronomical."

Are synthetic (manufactured) diamonds the same as natural diamonds?

Generally, gemological techniques can determine if a specimen is a natural diamond, a synthetic diamond, or a diamond simulant. However, it is not easy for the naked human eye to detect the difference.

How deep are diamond mines?

Diamonds form deep within the earth. However, they are sometimes brought close to the surface by volcanic eruptions. The deepest diamond mine is 1722 ft. (525 meters) deep. It is in Eastern Siberia, Russia. The diamonds found in the mine were formed at least 93 miles (150 kilometers) below the surface of the earth.

Do diamonds form from coal?

Diamonds are a very concentrated type of carbon (the same element that makes up coal). However, almost all diamonds were not formed from coal. The reason is that most diamonds are older than the carbon in coal that was formed from the first dead land plants. (The youngest diamonds are more than a billion years old.) More than 99 percent of diamonds are <u>older</u> than the first earth plants that formed coal.

Coal

How hard are diamonds?

Diamonds are the hardest natural material. They do not wear away and can only be scratched by other diamonds. This is the reason diamonds are very useful in industrial applications such as cutting, grinding, polishing, and drilling.

Diamond cutter

Which city is known as the "world diamond capital?"

The city of Antwerp (Belgium) is known as the world diamond capital. It processes 80% of all rough diamonds, more than 50% of cut diamonds and more than 50% of all rough and cut industrial diamonds.

In which city are most diamonds sold?

80% of the world's diamonds are sold in New York City.

What is the name of the world's largest diamond mining company

De Beers. It is the largest mine operator and largest distributor of gem quality diamonds.

What is the total amount of diamonds that have been mined so far?

The total amount of diamonds that have been mined so far is 500 tons (as compared to a total of 175,000 tons of gold).

Gold and Diamonds Mined

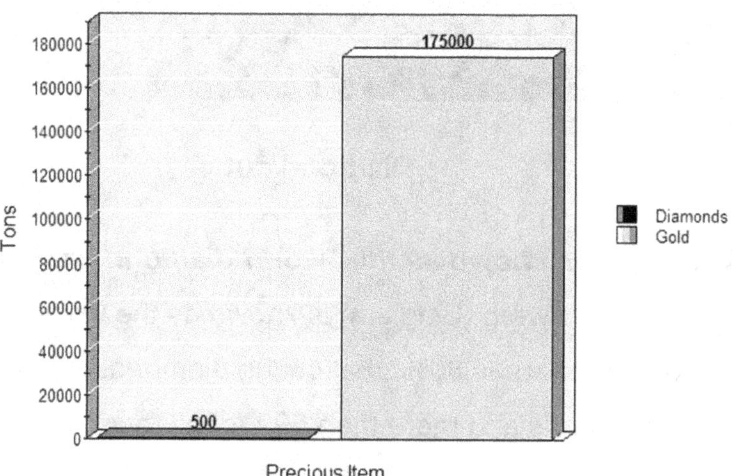

What quantity of diamonds is mined every year?

Approximately 57,000 pounds of diamonds are mined every year, valued at about 9 billion U.S. dollars (7,256,520 Euros).

What are the top 10 natural diamond producing countries?

In 2009, the top 10 diamond producing countries were (in descending order):

1. Russia
2. Canada
3. Botswana
4. Angola
5. South Africa
6. Namibia
7. Australia
8. Congo
9. Lesotho
10. Sierra Leone

Other countries include:

11. Central African Republic
12. Guinea
13. Tanzania
14. Zimbabwe
15. Guyana
16. Liberia
17. Ghana
18. Republic of Congo
19. India
20. Brazil
21. Indonesia
22. China

What is an "irradiated diamond?"

An irradiated diamond is a diamond which has undergone artificial irradiation with the aim of enhancing its optical properties. The irradiation changes the atomic structure of the diamond, thereby decreasing the visibility of its inclusions. Irradiation also creates gemstones of colors that do not exist in nature. A colorless diamond, or a yellow to brown diamond, that is irradiated can change color from green to blue.

What are birthstones?

Birthstones are 12 gems that are popularly associated with the 12 months of the year, with a different one for the month during which a person was born.

January: Garnet	July: Ruby
February: Amethyst	August: Peridot
March: Aquamarine	September: Sapphire
April: Diamond	October: Tourmaline or Opal
May: Emerald	November: Topaz or Citrine
June: Pear or Alexandrite	December: Tanzanite, Zircon, or Turquoise

---

Birthstones are also associated with the <u>12 Zodiacal signs</u>.

Sign	Dates	Stone
Aquarius	21 Jan. - 18 Feb.	garnet
Pisces	19 Feb. - 20 March	amethyst
Aries	21 March - 20 April	bloodstone
Taurus	21 April - 21 May	sapphire
Gemini	22 May - 21 June	agate
Cancer	21 June - 22 July	emerald
Leo	23 July - 22 August	onyx
Virgo	23 Aug. - 22 Sept.	carnelian
Libra	23 Sept. - 23 Oct.	chrysolite
Scorpio	24 Oct. - 21 Nov.	beryl
Sagittarius	22 Nov. - 21 Dec.	topaz
Capricorn	22 Dec. - 21 Jan.	ruby

In addition to the above, according to some astrologers, diamond is the gemstone for those who are born under Virgo and Libra.

History

Diamonds were first harvested in India, perhaps as early as 6,000 years ago.

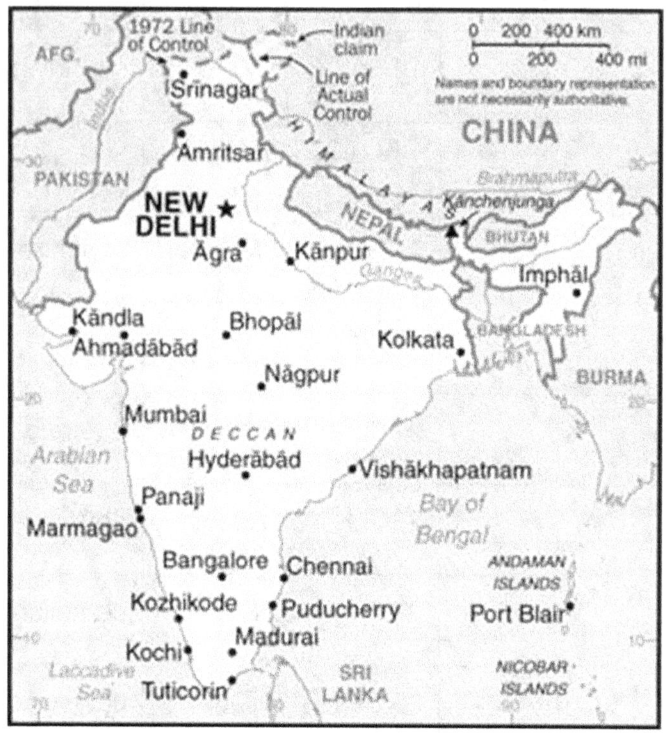

Rich concentrations of diamonds were discovered in the flood deposits along the rivers of Krishna, Penner, and Godavari. Diamonds were also collected from other rivers and streams. Historians estimate that trading of diamonds for India's wealthy nobles was perhaps done as early as the fourth century BC.

References to diamonds can be found in ancient Sanskrit texts. Buddhist writings from the 4th century BC also mention diamonds, and Indian scripts from the 3rd century praise the qualities of diamonds. A 3rd century BC Chinese work mentions diamonds worn by foreigners.

Pliny the Elder, a Roman writer, wrote in the first century AD about the ornamental and engraving uses of diamonds.

"Diamond is the most valuable, not only of precious stones, but of all things in the world."

In ancient times, diamonds were primarily used as engraving tools and religious icons. However, by the fourteenth century diamonds became fashionable accessories for the European elite. As early as the 15th century, European aristocracy was using diamonds for engagement rings, in addition to ruby and sapphire.

By the 1700s, Brazil became an important supplier of diamonds. For more than 150 years, it dominated the diamond market. In the 1800s, diamonds were discovered in South Africa. Some say that this marked the beginning of the modern diamond market.

Large scale diamond mining can be traced back to the 1860s, in Kimberley, South Africa. In 1888 the British explorer, Cecil Rhodes, along with Charles Rudd, consolidated some smaller companies and founded the present De Beers mining company. Today De Beers provides about a third of the total yearly world supply of diamonds.

Cecil Rhodes

By the 1970s, the most important producers of diamonds were South Africa, the Democratic Republic of Congo, and the Soviet Union.

The popularity of diamonds has been significantly influenced by a major publicity campaign by De Beers that started in the 1930s. The campaign established diamonds as a status symbol and as an important part of the betrothal process. The campaign, plus the industry's managed supply, have succeeded in maintaining the value of gem diamonds.

Today, the yearly production of diamonds is about 130 million carats.

1. about 92% are cut and polished in India
2. about 50% of cut diamonds and 40% of industrial diamonds are traded in Belgium.

"Blood diamonds" are diamonds used to promote illegal purposes, including armed conflict and civil wars in Africa. Some diamond retailers refuse to deal in conflict diamonds ("blood diamonds").

Natural Diamonds

In contemporary society, the use of diamonds has spread to the scientific field and the general jewelry market.

The popularity of gem diamonds is mostly due to their hardness and their high ability to disperse light, which gives them their brilliant quality.

Natural diamonds (without impurities) are colorless and almost transparent.

Natural "rough" diamond

Impurities in the diamond (one part per million of other types of atoms atoms) adds color to diamonds. Nitrogen atoms can give a yellow or brown color. Boron atoms make the diamond appear blue. Some other colors of diamonds are: green, purple, pink, orange, and red.

The International Diamond Council oversees diamond grading.

Diamonds are weighed, and their weight is expressed in "carats." One carat is equal to 200 milligrams.

Diamonds have a high ability to disperse light of different colors.

"Black" (Carbonado diamonds) have many dark inclusions that produce the dark color.

The 28 registered diamond exchanges in the world are called *bourses*.

Diamonds

The following is one estimate of the average pricing structure of jewelry diamonds:

> The value of one year's production of raw diamonds:
> **9 billion (US)**
>
> After cutting and polishing:
> **14 billion (US)**
>
> Wholesale price:
> **28 billion (US)**
>
> Retail price:
> **57 billion (US)**

Generally, factors that play a role in the markup of diamonds and other precious stones by a retail jeweler include: volume and speed of sales, the jeweler's typical client, and location.

<u>Some high prices paid for diamonds</u>

Diamond	Year sold	Carats	Price
Oppenheimer Blue	2016	14.62 carats (2.924 g) world's largest blue diamond	auctioned at Christie's (Geneva) for $50.6 million.
Blue Moon of Josephine	2015	12.03 carats	Sotheby's auction for $48.4 million
Pink Star	2013	59.60 carats (11.920 g)	Auctioned in Geneva by Sotheby's for $83.17 million
Archduke Joseph	2012	76.02 carats colorless	sold by Christie for $21.4 million
Martian Pink	2012	12.04 carats	sold at auction for $17 million
blue diamond	2009	7.03 carat, (1.406 g)	$9.5 million, at auction

Diamonds

Diamond	Year sold	Carats	Price
pink diamond	2009	5 carats, (1.0 g)	$10.8 million, sold in Hong Kong
Wittelsbach diamond	2008	35.56 carat, (7.112 g)	$24 million at Christie's auction
Star of the Season	1995	100.10 carats (20.020 g)	$16.55 million at Sotheby's auction

Sotheby's is a multinational corporation and one of the world's biggest brokers of jewelry, art, real estate and collectibles. It is headquartered in New York City and has 90 locations in 40 countries.

Christie's is a large British auction house. It was founded in 1766 and has main offices in London and New York City. It has the distinction of selling the Salvador Mundi for $450.3 US million, the most ever paid for a painting.

Jewelry Diamonds

The yearly amount of diamonds that is mined is 57,320 pounds (25,999 kilograms), or 130,000000 carats, Generally, only 20% of mined diamonds are suitable for jewelry.

In mines, diamonds are located by using X-ray fluorescent lights.

Diamond mining

One of the most productive diamond mines is the *Jwaneng mine* in Botswana. Alluvial (flood) diamond deposits also account for a significant portion of diamonds and are found in many places, such as the alluvial deposits in Brazil.
The top three diamond mining sites are:

    1. Botswana (24 million carats)

    2. Russia (17.8 million carats)

3. Diavik Diamond mine in Canada (10.9 million carats)

Diamonds

Most diamonds are cut and polished in just a few centers. The biggest center is in Surat, India.

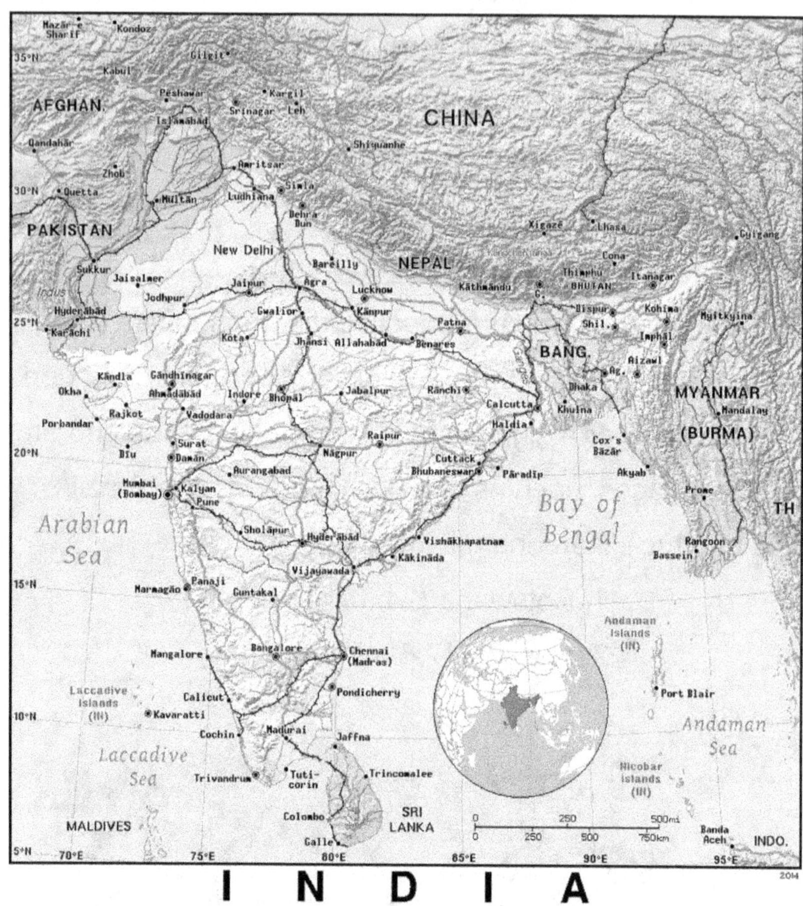

Other centers are:

Antwerp diamond district (Belgium)

London (England)

Diamond District (New York)

Diamond Exchange District (Tel Aviv)

<u>The four "Cs"</u>

Although there are many diamond characteristics, the grading of gem grade diamonds is usually done by evaluating the "four Cs" (major <u>C</u>haracteristics of diamonds).

1. <u>Carat</u> (<u>not</u> *carrot* - is the diamond's <u>weight</u>)
   Interestingly, diamonds that are "shy" of whole and half carat marks (Example: .9 carat diamonds instead of 1.0 carat diamonds) are often available at significantly lower prices.

2. <u>Cut quality</u> (proportions, symmetry, and polish)
   Of the four characteristics of diamonds, "cut quality" is the only one which is mostly determined by man and not mother nature. Optimum cutting of the diamond increases its "brilliance" - and market value.

3. <u>Color</u> (whiteness or colorless, and the intensity of its hue)
   Higher "color grades" refer to <u>less</u> color of the diamond.

4. <u>Clarity</u> (Clarity refers to the degree of freedom from inclusions (any material trapped inside the diamond.) Higher grade diamonds have less inclusions. Because most inclusions are microscopic, they usually do not affect the visible beauty of the diamond.

<u>Shapes of Diamonds</u>

Rough diamonds are cut into many shapes ("fancy cuts") to increase the beauty and market value.

Generally, rough diamonds lose about fifty percent of their bulk as a result of the cutting process..

The style of cuts has evolved through the ages.

The following are some of the major traditional diamond shapes

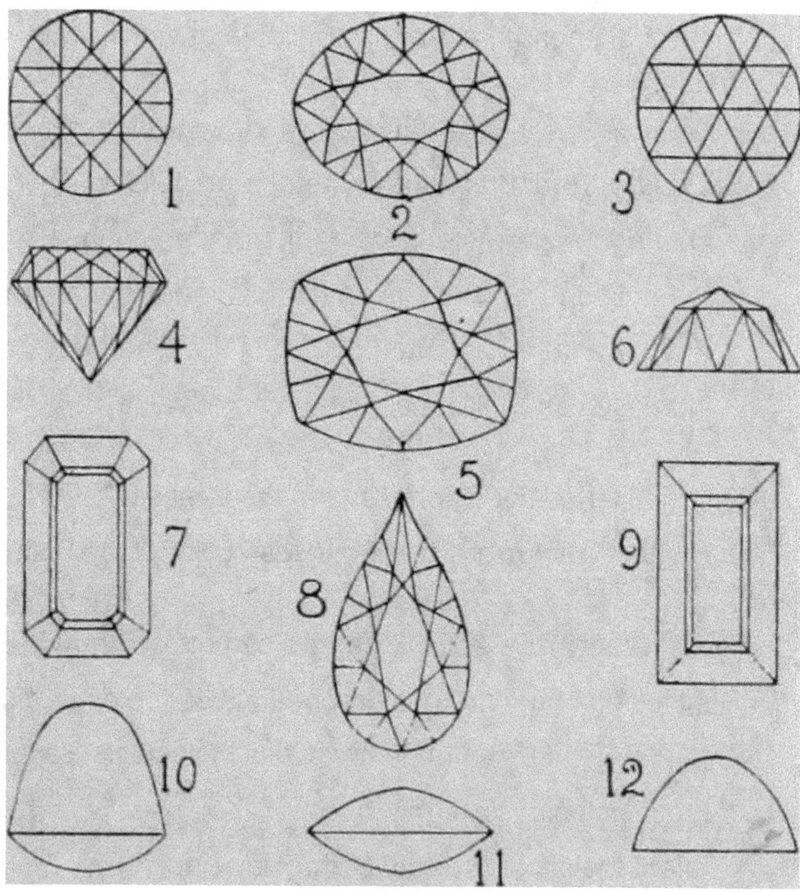

<u>Number 1: Round</u>
(the most popular shape.)

Number 1: The "Round cut" has 58 facets on the crown (the upper part of the diamond) and 25 on the pavilion (the part of the diamond cut below the girdle).

Number	Diamond cut
1	Round brilliant, top view
2	Oval brilliant, top view
3	Rose cut, top view
4	Round brilliant, side view
5	Custom brilliant, top view
6	Rose cut, side view
7	Step cut, octagon
8	Pear brilliant, top view
9	Step cut, oblong
10	High cabochon, side view
11	Cabochon, side view
12	Lentil-shaped, side view

<u>Contemporary diamond styles include:</u>

Paul Noillimrev

<u>Princess</u>

The princess cut was developed in the 1960s. The top of the diamond (the face-up part) is usually square. The side is in the shape of an inverted pyramid. It is usually cheaper than a round diamond.

<u>Asscher</u>

The Asscher cut was introduced in 1902 and was the first signature cut to be patented. The diamond looks square. However, with all four corners cropped, it is more octagonal. Although this cut was somewhat popular in the 1900s, it surged in popularity during the early 2000s.

<u>Marquise</u>

The marquise cut diamond is football shaped (or, eye-shaped, or boat shaped). It was developed in the 20th century and has 58 facets.

<u>Radiant</u>

Radiant cut diamonds are like princess cut diamonds. However, they are usually rectangular as opposed to square and less popular than the princess cut diamonds.

Heart

In 1562 Queen Elizabet reocived a heart-shaped diamond gift from Mary Queen of Scots as a symbol of friendship and goodwill. Heart-shaped diamonds are the most expensive type of cut diamonds.

Cushion

Cushion-cut diamonds have a square cut with rounded corners (making them resemble a pillow). They are cut shallow, causing a lack of brilliance. Because of this, they are usually priced 25-50% lower than round brilliant diamonds.

> "Zsa Zsa Gabor was once asked whether a lady should return the ring after cancelling an engagement. She answered, "Of course, darling, but first, you take out all the diamonds."
> *- Zsa Zsa Gabor*
> *Hungarian-American actress*

Diamond Cutting

Major diamond cutting centers are in Antwerp, Amsterdam, Johannesburg, New York City, and Tel Aviv.
The larger and therefore more valuable diamonds are usually processed in North America and Europe.

Although diamonds are extremely hard, they can be split by a single blow. Diamond cutters ("lapidaries") are well trained and use a combination of skills, experience and scientific knowledge to produce finished diamonds with different facets (the flat sides of diamonds). Some diamond shapes are: round, pear, marquise, oval, and hearts.

After cutting, diamonds are polished and then examined for possible flaws and correction procedures such as re-polishing and different arrangements in the jewelry.

The rough diamond yearly production is 130 million carats (with 92% cut and polished in India).

The popularity of cuts usually varies with fashion.

<u>Diamond Marketing</u>

"A diamond is forever" and other slogans, in addition to intense marketing campaigns, have succeeded in increasing the diamond market in many countries, and creating new markets.

A major factor in diamond marketing is diamond certification, done by "diamond certifiers" - organizations that provide grading services. Although there are hundreds of such organizations, there are two main ones:

1. The GIA (Gemological Institute of America)
2. The EGL (European Gemological Laboratory)

Diamond grading is subjective. More than one person examines the diamond for the four major qualities: carat, color, clarity, and cut. After inspection, a certificate is issued showing proof of the quality and authenticity of the diamond.

It is important to understand the difference between certifications and appraisals. As stated above, certifications are done by grading services. Appraisals, on the other hand, are done by jewelers. The certification may list information regarding the manufacturing of the diamond, and the weight and metals used in the gem piece.

Industrial Diamonds

Diamond is the hardest "bulk" material (material found in loose form).

Industrial diamonds make up about 80 percent of mined diamonds.

Diamond tipped scraper

Industrial diamonds have more flaws and quality-reducing color than jewel-quality diamonds and are therefore used in cutting and polishing tools and industrial abrasives.

Also, because of their high thermal conductivity, industrial diamonds are used as "heat sinks" in the production of some integrated circuits.

The top 5 producers of natural industrial diamond-producing countries are:

1. Russia (18 million carats)
2. Australia (13 million carats)
3. Democratic Republic of the Congo (11 million carats)
4. Botswana (6 million carats)
5. South Africa (4 million carats)

<u>Synthetic Diamonds</u>

Synthetic diamonds are known by different names: artificial diamonds, cultured diamonds, cultivated diamonds. They are created in a laboratory by an artificial process, as opposed to natural diamonds which are created by geologic processes.

In 1955 General Electric was successful in creating diamonds from graphite. These diamonds had industrial applications (grinding, drilling, etc.).

With recent scientific advancements, synthetic diamonds of significant size can now be manufactured. These synthetic diamonds are identical to natural diamonds on a molecular level, except that they have noticeably different crystal patterns. Also, natural diamonds have superior thermal conductivity and can be distinguished from synthetic diamonds by a 2-3 second test using electronic thermal probes.

Synthetic diamonds can be produced in as little as three months. One process applies high temperature and pressure. Another process is similar in approach to a 3-D printing system, with individual layers of carbon deposited or "printed" one on top of the other.

Two main processes used to create synthetic diamonds are:

1. HPHT (high pressure high temperature process), and

2. CVD (chemical vapor deposition crystal formation method).

Approximately 98 percent of industrial diamonds are synthetic diamonds.

About 90 percent of synthetic diamonds are produced in China.

In 2014 the amount of synthetic diamonds that was produced was 4,500,000,000 carats 1,984,160 pounds (900,000 kg).

Clear white, yellow, brown, blue, green and orange diamonds can be produced by both the HPHT and CVD methods. They can all be cut into gems.

Most synthetic diamonds are produced by the HPHT method.

Diamond simulants look like diamonds and have some diamond qualities. The term "diamante" refers to these diamond simulants. "Diamond-like carbon," has some qualities of diamonds and is used to coat and thereby enhance diamond simulants.

Another diamond simulant (silicon carbide) or "moissanite." is more expensive than cubic zirconia.

BARS apparatus

The "BARS" creates the high pressure and high-temperature environment required to grow diamonds.

It was invented in 1989-1991 by the Siberian Branch of the Academy of Sciences of the USSR.

<u>Cubic Zirconia</u>

Cubic Zirconia is the most common diamond simulant. It is the crystalline form of zirconium dioxide. First produced in 1976, it looks very much like a diamond, but is inexpensive. For example, a one carat cubic zirconia gemstone retails for approximately $20 dollars, as opposed to a one carat diamond which retails for about $1,500 dollars.

<u>Properties of Cubic Zirconia</u>

Quality	Cubic Zirconia	Diamond
Hardness	8 on Mohs hardness scale	10
Specific gravity (density)	1.7 (that of diamond)	1.0
Refractive index	2.15-2.18	2.42
Dispersion	0.058-0.066	0.044
Cut	edges may be cut rounded or smooth	usually sharp edges
Color	colorless (but may be produced with colors)	Only rare diamonds are colorless.
Thermal conductivity	thermal insulator	thermal conductor

Famous Diamonds

The Cullinan Diamond

The Cullinan Diamond (3,106 carats, 621.35 g.) is the largest rough diamond ever discovered (1905). "Cullinan" was the name of the chairman of the diamond mine. The rough diamond was cut into several gems, one of which (530.4 carats, 106.08 g.) forms part of the British "Sovereign's Scepter with Cross". Another part, the "Star of Africa" (317. carats, 63.48 g.), forms part of "Imperial State Crown". Both cut diamonds are part of the British Crown Jewels and can be viewed at the Tower of London. Seven other parts (208.29 carats) are privately owned by Queen Elizabeth II.

Hope Diamond

This diamond is 45.52 carats (9.104 g) and is fancy dark greyish-blue in color. The original larger stone (about 112 carats) originated in India and was purchased by a French Merchant in 1666. After a succession of owners, including Henry Philip Hop, who owned the diamond in the 1830's, it was purchased by gem merchant Harry Winston, who donated it to the National Museum of Natural History in 1958. Estimated value is $200-$250 million dollars.

The Taylor-Burton

Discovered in 1966 in the Premier Mine in South Africa, the rough stone (240.80 carats), was cut into a pear-shaped diamond (69.42 carats, 13.6 g.) It was bought by actor Richard Burton ($1.1 million) and given as an engagement ring to Elizabeth Taylor. After Richard Burton's death, Elizabeth Taylor sold the stone (2.8 million) and donated the proceeds to a hospital in Biafra.

26th Congress of the Communist Party of the Soviet Union

This yellow diamond of 342.57 g. (uncut weight) is the largest ever found in Russia. Mined in 1980, it is the size of a pigeon's egg and is kept in the Russian Diamond Fund (Moscow).

Amarillo Starlight

This is the largest diamond found in the Crater of Diamonds State Park in Amarillo, Arkansas. It was found in 1975 by W.W. Johnson while vacationing in the park with his family. It has a cut weight of 1.508 g. and is valued at approximately $150,000 - $175,000.

Sweet Josephine and Blue Moon of Josephine

The Sweet Josephine is a pink, cushion-shaped "fancy vivid" stone. In November 2015 it was bought at a Christie's auction in Geneva by Hong Kong billionaire Joseph Lau for his 7 years-old daughter. The estimated price is $23-28 million. It is a cushion shaped diamond of more than 10 carats and one of only three diamonds of such weight to be purchased at auction during the previous 250 years.

The following day at Sotheby's, Joseph Lau also bought "The Blue Moon of Josephine" for his daughter for $48.4 million, US. It is a 12.03 carat (2.406 g) blue diamond. This diamond is the largest "fancy vivid" cushion-shaped blue stone ever to be auctioned off.

> "I thought of the soul as resembling a castle, formed of a single diamond or a very transparent crystal, and containing many rooms...."
>
> - *Saint Theresa of Avila*

Crater of Diamonds State Park

Crater of Diamonds State Park, in the U.S. state of Arkansas, offers people a unique opportunity to search for diamonds in an area that has been proven to contain diamonds.

The first time that diamonds were found in the Crater of Diamonds area was in 1906, by the owner of the farmland, John Wesley Huddleston. Today the land is owned by the Arkansas Parks Department.

Treasure hunters can search for diamonds in the 37.5-acre site for a small fee - and they are permitted to keep any diamond that they find!

<u>Some famous recent finds in the park</u>

2006: The Sunshine Diamond - 5.47 carats

2009: The Arabian Knight - 5.75 carats

2011: The Illusion Diamond - 8.66 carats

2015: The Esperanza Diamond - 8.52 carats

Danaptik

Crater of Diamonds State Park

<u>Feeling lucky?</u>

Visit: www.CraterofDiamondsStatePark.com

Diamonds as an investment

The resale of diamonds is not as clear-cut as the resale of gold or silver. For example, two ounces of gold are usually worth two times the value of one ounce of gold. However, a two-carat diamond may be worth four times the value of a one carat diamond - or it may be worth a different amount, depending on many factors such as color (whiteness or colorless, and the intensity of its hue), cut quality (proportions, symmetry, and polish), and clarity (degree of freedom from inclusions, which is any material trapped inside the diamond).

Another market pricing factor to consider is the difficulty in distinguishing between synthetic diamonds and naturally occurring diamonds and the lack of one centralized market. In addition, some jurisdictions may impose sales tax or value-added tax. All these factors may affect the market price of diamonds.

One must also keep in mind that many diamonds are sold by retail stores which markup the diamonds for a very high profit. Sometimes overcoming this "markup gap" and earning a profit on the sale of a diamond is a difficult task.

The possibility of diamonds (naturally occurring or synthetic) flooding the market must also be considered. The general law of supply and demand suggests this would decrease the market value of most diamonds.

Recent Diamond News

A welcomed shower

Scientists have conducted studies which indicate that it rains diamonds on the planets Neptune and Jupiter.

A novel addition

Researchers have discovered that adding nano-sized diamonds to the electrolyte in lithium batteries inhibits the creation of "dendrites" in the batteries and therefore allows batteries with more lithium. The nano-diamonds also decrease the number of battery malfunctions, such as fires in smartphones.

Growing diamonds

A new company, "Diamond Foundry," is getting attention for growing diamonds by a process known as "chemical vapor deposition." In a chamber the size of a bowling ball, a diamond "seed" is exposed to chemicals, including hydrogen and gaseous form of carbon. Then, in temperatures hotter than the sun, the diamond grows - like in the "grow a crystal" children science kits. The rough diamond is then cut by professional diamond cutters and is allegedly indistinguishable from real diamonds.

<u>Legal knock-offs?</u>

A 2018 article in the New York Times spoke of the increased availability of synthetic diamonds and the effect that it might have on diamond popularity and sales. Some jewelry stores sell synthetic diamonds at a price that is 30 to 40 percent less than natural diamonds. These jewelry stores allegedly clearly label these diamonds as synthetic. Also, the company that grows them inscribes each diamond by laser that it is a synthetically grown diamond.

The article points out that synthetic diamonds may have less of a resale value than natural diamonds and that many diamonds (both natural and synthetic) cannot necessarily be guaranteed to be a store of value.

<u>A piercing innovation</u>

Can you believe that some people, including Millennials are replacing engagement rings with diamonds embedded in their fingers? A recent feature by CBS news reported that the $100 procedure is usually performed by a piercing artist and takes about ten minutes.

"A piercing artist marks the spot with a pen, cleans with alcohol and iodine, uses a tool to remove a small patch of skin, and then inserts an anchor made of titanium or gold, which holds the gem," said Cindy Hsu, the CBS reporter.

The procedure is a bit painful and can lead to complications. However, it can be reversed, confirming that diamonds are not necessarily forever.

Still hot from the mine

In March 2018, the "Lesotho Legend" a 910-carat diamond, sold for $40 million dollars, US. The diamond, recovered from the Letseng mine in Lesotho, a southern African country and is the world's fifth largest diamond gem, the size of two golf balls.

In September 2017, a rough diamond from Botswana, sold for $53 million dollars, US. That diamond is the biggest uncut diamond found during the last 100 years.

Eye-catching video

In the Taylor Swift video "Look What You Made Me Do," Taylor Swift takes a "diamond bath" in a tub filled with real jewels worth more than $10 million dollars, US. Celebrity jeweler Neil Lane commented, "...diamonds have never looked better!"

I've got ants (no - *diamonds*) in my pants

On January 19, 2018 a man was arrested in Paris with more than 250,000 Euros of diamonds in his pants. There were hundreds of uncut diamonds neatly packed in plastic packets and hidden in his undergarments. It is thought that he was transporting them from the Democratic Republic of the Congo to Paris.

Diamond-coated implants

Some scientists say that titanium implants coated with fine diamonds (just a few millionths of a centimeter long) will prove to be more comfortable than current versions - and less infection-prone. The diamonds are cheap and take just several minutes to create.

In thirteenth century France, it was illegal for anyone other than the King to wear diamonds.

Diamond Myths

All diamonds are naturally created by mother nature.

During the Middle Ages, it was believed that to protect a house from lightning or storm, a diamond had to be situated at each corner of the house.

The Titanic sank because of the presence of the Hope diamond aboard the ship.

In the Middle Ages and the Renaissance, diamond rings were believed to have the power to ward off devils, nightmares, and savage beasts.

Also, in the Middle Ages, diamonds were thought able to impart virtue and generosity and heal the sick.

Diamonds cannot have surfaces that are curved.

Diamonds do not conduct electricity.

Diamonds are forever. (Although they do not last forever due to degradation to graphite, the degradation process can take billions of years...almost forever?)

"I never worry about diets. The only carrots that interest me are the number of carats in a diamond."
                                                  - Mae West

"The diamond has always been esteemed by the ancients the rarest stone, and the most precious of all, its fine brilliancy, its water, or its virtues....it calms anger and foments love between man and wife and is therefore called the stone of reconciliation."
                                                  - Lewis Vertoman

<u>Interesting Facts About Diamonds</u>

Diamonds were once used in India to keep away evil spirits and to cure diseases. However, about six hundred years ago, the Archduke Maximillian of Austria gave a diamond ring to Mary of Burgundy when he asked her to be his wife. Although it was not the first time that a diamond ring was used for such purpose, it popularized the act.

The most famous use of gem diamonds is for engagement rings. The great majority of people in the world easily recognize a diamond ring as a symbol of being engaged for marriage.

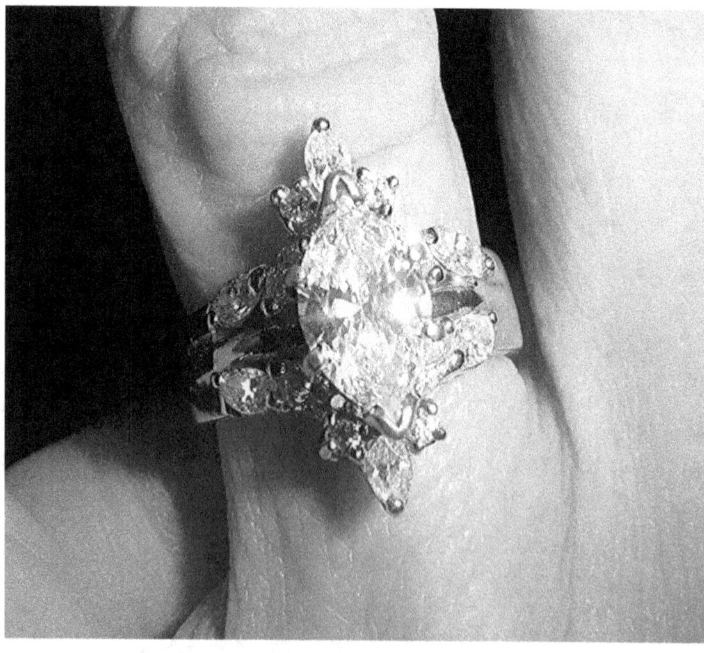

Some diamonds are colorless. Others may be yellow, brown, gray, green, blue, pink, violet, orange, red, purple (and even black). The color of a diamond is often a result of defects in the crystal lattice or chemical impurities.

Black diamonds (Carbonado diamonds) is the toughest form of natural diamonds. They are priced less than clear diamonds. Some think that these diamonds were formed by meteorite impacts.

The biggest "perfect" diamond is known as "The Paragon". It is the tenth largest diamond in the world and weighs 137.82 carats (27.564 g.) It is flawless and without inclusions.

You personally can mine for diamonds! The Crater of Diamonds State Park in Arkansas is the only mine in the world open for the public to dig up diamonds. Diamonds have been discovered there since 1906. For more information, visit www.CraterofDiamondsStatePark.com

But why mine for diamonds when you can just scoop them up? Scientists at the Stanford Linear Accelerator Center (SLAC) have conducted studies which suggest that the atmospheres of Neptune and Jupiter are just right for the creation of diamonds in their atmospheres. Therefore, when we visit these two planets, we should remember to take with us sturdy "diamond umbrellas."

However, we don't have to settle for just diamond rain. There's another world, "55 Cancri E," where scientists think that the entire mantle of the planet is made up of diamonds!

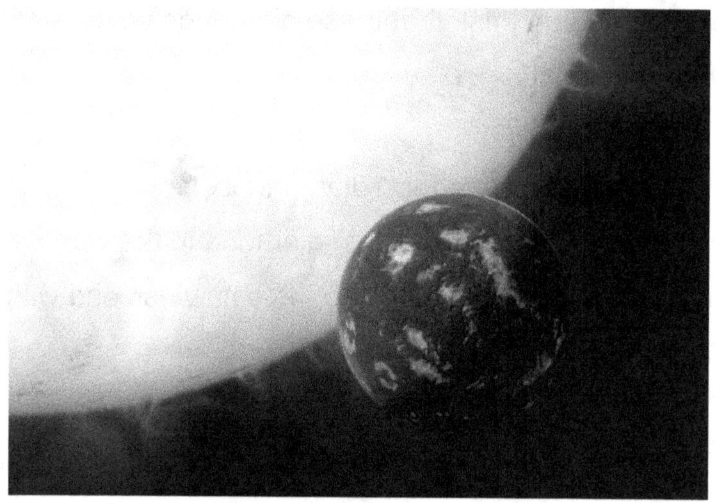

55 Cancri E   ESA/HUBBLE

Currently, synthetic diamonds represent about 2% of gem-quality diamonds and 98% of industrial diamonds. Diamonds and coal are similar. However, the atoms in diamonds are arranged differently than the atoms in coal. This gives diamonds their characteristic appearance and qualities.

Some diamonds may have been brought to earth by meteorites!

Diamonds

Diamonds were once thought to possess healing qualities. They were considered a "miracle stone' with the ability to cure infections, skin diseases, memory loss, nightmares, heart ailments, and a variety of other maladies.

Diamonds are tough compared to other gemstones. However, a diamond can break if hit hard by a hammer. Also, diamonds can be burned at temperatures from about 1290 to 1650 Fahrenheit (698 to 899 Celsius).

Diamonds come in all rainbow colors.

North America produces about 10 percent of the world's diamonds.

More than 50% of the world's gem quality diamonds are bought in the United States. However, it only produces about one percent of the earth's supply.
The Hindus believed that diamonds were created by lightning hitting the earth.

Rings that are given as tokens of love or as a symbol of marriage are worn on the fourth finger because it was believed that a vein flows from there to the heart.

Diamonds

Today diamonds are mined in all continents except two: Europe and Antarctica.

A "paragon" is a perfect diamond (without flaws and inclusions) that is at least 100 carats (20 g.)

Scientists think that some white dwarf stars have diamond cores. The biggest one is believed to weigh 2.27 trillion tons!

Long ago, Jewish priests used diamonds to judge a person accused of a crime. They held a diamond in front of the person and observed whether the diamond dulled or shined. Dullness meant the person was guilty. A shine indicated the person was innocent.

Ancient Romans believed that diamonds were the tears of the gods.

"A diamond in the rough" refers to an individual of fine character who presently lack refined manners and graces.

Diamond is the birthstone of the month of April and the gemstone for the state of Arkansas (US).

One of the four C's of diamonds is "carat" - a unit of mass equal to 200 milligrams. The word is derived from "carob" seeds which were used as a unit of measurement in ancient history. "Carats" have been used to measure the weights of diamonds since the 1570's.

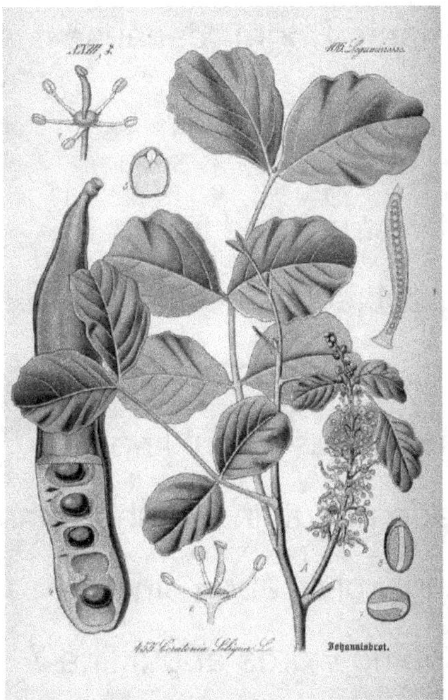

Carob tree and seeds

The first playing cards were developed in China more than 1,000 years ago. Diamonds were not one of the original suits.

Diamond Poem (Diamante Poem)

The diamond poem was developed by Iris Tiedt in *A New Poetry Form: The Diamante* (1969). It is referred to as a "Diamante Poem" because it is diamond-shaped.

It consists of 7 structured lines:

1: Beginning subject

2: Two describing words about line 1

3: Three doing words about line 1

4: Short phrase about line 1, short phrase about line 7

5: Three doing words about line 7

6: Two describing words about line 7

7: End subject

Diamante Poem

Love

selfless, forever

understanding, caring, protecting,

unexpected great happiness, astounding mystery

dedication, vigilance, attention

undefinable, challenging

life

Diamond Books

Fiction

Diamonds are Forever
(Ian Fleming, 1956)

James Bond infiltrates a smuggling ring, with locations from Sierra Leone to Las Vegas.

"An international diamond-smuggling pipeline has opened up and the British Treasury wants to know who's controlling it. Impersonating a captured courier named Peter Franks, Bond infiltrates the criminal ring and finds an unlikely ally in Tiffany Case, a gorgeous American with a dark past. As the ring's stateside go-between, she may be just another link in the chain, but Tiffany is also Bond's best shot at finding the elusive figure at the head of the operation—a syndicate boss known only by the initials "ABC." But if Bond's cover gets blown, he'll find that the only thing harder than a diamond is surviving the payback of a pair of murderous henchmen.

"With a sparkling trail of smuggled gems as bait, *Diamonds Are Forever* leads Bond on a globe-hopping mission where deadly assassins lurk behind every corner."(1)

Master of the Game
(Sydney Sheldon, 1982)

Four generations, a diamond theft, and a thick plot.

Kate Blackwell "...is the symbol of success, the beautiful woman who parlayed her inheritance into an international conglomerate. Winner of a unique position among the wealthy and world-renowned. And she's a survivor, indomitable as her father, the man who returned from the edge of death to wrench a fortune in diamonds from the bleak South African earth. Now, celebrating her ninetieth birthday, Kate surveys the family she has manipulated, dominated, and loved: the fair and the grotesque, the mad and the mild, the good and the evil -- her winnings in life. Is she the...MASTER OF THE GAME?"(1)

The Devil's Star
(Joe Nesbo, 2003)

"Detective Harry Hole is on the trail of a diabolical serial killer terrorizing Oslo in another electrifying thriller in the Harry Hole series from the author of The Snowman.

"It's fascinating to watch this Norwegian author adapt our homegrown monster [the serial killer] to a foreign culture.... When things go wrong, Harry goes on a bender, but when he's on his game, no one is better than this obsessive detective. He systematically works his way through the intricacies of a plot that speeds along like a bullet train."—New York Times Book Review

"In the heat of a sweltering Oslo summer, a young woman is found murdered in her flat—with one of her fingers cut off and a tiny red star-shaped diamond placed under her eyelid. An off-the-rails alcoholic barely holding on to his job, Detective Harry Hole is assigned to the case with Tom Waaler, a hated colleague whom Harry believes is responsible for the murder of his partner. When another woman is reported missing five days later, and her severed finger turns up adorned with a red star-shaped diamond ring, Harry fears a serial killer is at work.

"But Hole's determination to capture a fiend and to expose Waaler's crimes is leading him into shadowy places where both investigations merge in unexpected ways, forcing him to make difficult decisions about a future he may not live to see."(1)

———————

Kill me if you can
(James Patterson and Marshall Karp, 2012)

"Matthew Bannon, a poor art student living in New York City, finds a duffel bag filled with diamonds during a chaotic attack at Grand Central Station. Plans for a worry-free life with his stunning girlfriend Katherine fill his thoughts--until he realizes that he is being hunted, and that whoever is after him won't stop until they have reclaimed the diamonds and exacted their revenge.

"Trailing him is the Ghost, the world's greatest assassin, who has just pulled off his most high-profile hit: killing Walter Zelvas, a top member of the international Diamond Syndicate. There's only one small problem: the diamonds he was supposed to retrieve from Zelvas are missing. Now, the Ghost is on Bannon's trail--but so is a rival assassin who would like nothing more than to make the Ghost disappear forever. From "America's #1 storyteller" (Forbes) comes a high-speed, high-stakes, winner-take-all thrill ride of adrenaline-fueled suspense."(1)

The Engagements
(J. Courtney Sullivan, 2013)

"From the New York Times best-selling author of Commencement and Maine comes a gorgeous, sprawling novel about marriage—about those who marry in a white heat of passion, those who marry for partnership and comfort, and those who live together, love each other, and have absolutely no intention of ruining it all with a wedding.

"Evelyn has been married to her husband for forty years—forty years since he slipped off her first wedding ring and put his own in its place. Delphine has seen both sides of love—the ecstatic, glorious highs of seduction, and the bitter, spiteful fury that descends when it's over. James, a paramedic who works the night shift, knows his wife's family thinks she could have done better; while Kate, partnered with Dan for a decade, has seen every kind of wedding—beach weddings, backyard weddings, castle weddings—and has vowed never, ever, to have one of her own.

"As these lives and marriages unfold in surprising ways, we meet Frances Gerety, a young advertising copywriter in 1947. Frances is working on the De Beers campaign and she needs a signature line, so, one night before bed, she scribbles a phrase on a scrap of paper: "A Diamond Is Forever." And that line changes everything.

"A rich, layered, exhilarating novel spanning nearly a hundred years, The Engagements captures four wholly unique marriages, while tracing the story of diamonds in America, and the way—for better or for worse—these glittering stones have come to symbolize our deepest hopes for everlasting love."(1)

Diamond Books

Non-fiction

Famous Diamonds
(Ian Balfour, 2008)

"The history of great diamonds is intimately interwoven with the lives of emperors and conquerors, great kings and queens, with statesmen and soldiers, the rich and famous - but also, inevitably, with those who lead more shadowy lives. Diamonds have been objects of passion, sometimes of war, violence and theft.

"As well as being objects of exceptional beauty and rarity, they were once thought to possess magical properties that protected their owners from enemies. Initially a male prerogative reflecting status and authority, these incredible gems later adorned the wives of powerful men, and at times were offered as influential gifts. Few were immune to the temptation of diamonds; many sacrificed their lives and souls to them.

"In Famous Diamonds, Ian Balfour tells the fascinating stories of almost 80 of these remarkable gems including the famous: Koh-i-Noor, which is set in the British Crown Jewels; the infamous: the deep blue Hope Diamond, which is said to bring bad luck to all who handle it; the biggest: The Cullinan; and the

Hollywood romantic: the Taylor-Burton Diamond. Some have detailed histories that can be traced from the present day back to the moment they were mined, while others have a more mysterious past or have disappeared from view. Also included are shorter entries on a further selection of some forty notable diamonds."(1)

Diamond Handbook
(Renee Newman, Second Edition, 2010)

More of interest to professionals and serious diamond buyers.

"This handbook updates jewellery professionals and serious diamond buyers on the new developments in diamond grading, treatments, synthetic diamonds, fancy-colour diamonds and lab certificates. Using close-up photographs, it shows how to make visual judgements about clarity, transparency, cut quality and brilliance. The handbook also discusses how gem labs are incorporating brightness, size, scintillation and pattern into their cut grades, and it provides tips on detecting treatments and man-made diamonds. Topics include: quality evaluation; diamond recutting; branded diamonds; antique cuts and jewellery; diamond treatments; fancy-colour diamonds; synthetic diamonds; light performance; fluorescence; and, lab reports."(1)

From Mine to Mistress
(Chaim Evan-Zohar, 2002)

Covers the progress of diamonds from the rough stone to the final polished gem and sale.

"Secrecy clouds the entire diamond industry; its inner workings are often unclear to corporate and governmental decision-makers. Moreover, the rapid globalization of the industry is impacting on corporate strategies, and producer-country governments are demanding domestic beneficiation. Meanwhile, the uncartelization of the traditional monopoly structure has enhanced competition, causing a traditionally fragmented value chain to reorganize through growth or consolidation.

"This book is about adding value in the diamond pipeline from the mine (upstream) to the retail consumer (on the downstream side). At each level of the value chain, the revenue optimization choices are discussed.

"What all decision-makers require is access to industry information, and an answer to their questions. While this book does not give all the answers, it describes the systems as they operate today, and identifies the interaction among all industry players. Taken in its entirety, this book will leave you with a wealth of information. It should be thought-provoking and

---

enhance your understanding of what it takes to perpetuate the Diamond Dream."(1)

Blood Diamonds
(Greg Campbell, 2002)

"Tracing the Deadly Path of the World's Most Precious Stones."

"First discovered in 1930, the diamonds of Sierra Leone have funded one of the most savage rebel campaigns in modern history. These "blood diamonds" are smuggled out of West Africa and sold to legitimate diamond merchants in London, Antwerp, and New York, often with the complicity of the international diamond industry. Eventually, these very diamonds find their way into the rings and necklaces and brides and spouses the world over.

"Blood Diamonds is the gripping tale of how diamond smuggling works, how the rebel war has effectively destroyed Sierra Leone and its people, and how the policies of the diamonds industry—institutionalized in the 1880s by the De Beers cartel—have allowed it to happen. Award-winning journalist Greg Campbell traces the deadly trail of these diamonds, many of which are brought to the world market by fanatical enemies. These repercussions of diamond smuggling are felt far beyond the borders of the poor and war-ridden country of Sierra Leone, and the consequences of overlooking this African tragedy are both shockingly deadly and unquestionably global.

"In this newly revised and expanded edition, investigative journalist Greg Campbell returns to West Africa ten years later to reveal how despite widespread exposure to the corruption and greed of the diamond trade, it continues unabated as the region struggles politically, ecologically, and economically."(1)

The Queen's Diamonds
(Hugh Roberts, 2012)

All about the diamonds in the collection of Her Majesty The Queen.

"The splendor and sparkle of the diamond is unmatched by that of any other gem in the world. As status symbols or emblems of endless love, diamonds have been worn, collected, and presented as lavish gifts since the earliest days of antiquity. Today, steady sales—and borrowed baubles on the arms of starlets—indicate that diamonds remain among the most sought-after gemstones. But few, if any, private collections surpass that of Queen Elizabeth II.

"The Queen's Diamonds takes readers on a tour of the magnificent royal inheritance of diamonds from Queen Adelaide in the 1830s to the present day. The book features more than seventy awe-inspiring pieces of jewelry from one of the finest collections in the world. With three hundred full-color photographs—many newly commissioned for the book—the dazzling display ranges from the flawless pink diamond presented to Princess Elizabeth, as she was then known, for her wedding in 1947 to nineteenth-century diamond diadems to the Cartier "Halo" tiara worn most recently by The Duchess of Cambridge at her wedding in April 2011. As informative as it is stunningly beautiful, the book includes information on many items of international importance and great historic significance.

"Published on the occasion of the Diamond Jubilee of Queen Elizabeth II, The Queen's Diamonds offers the first authorized account of this iconic and unparalleled collection of diamond jewelry. The photos superbly encapsulate the breathtaking beauty of the subjects, and the descriptions are packed with fascinating details."(1)

(1) Amazon.com book description

"Big girls need big diamonds."

- Elizabeth Taylor
American actress

<u>Diamond Quotes</u>

"Better a diamond with a flaw than a
pebble without."
> *- Confucius*
> *Chinese philosopher*

"Invest in the human soul. Who knows, it might be a diamond in
the rough."
> *- Mary McLeod Bethune*
> *Civil rights activist*

"When there's pressure, I believe people will break under it or a
diamond will be created."
> *- Brock Osweiler*
> *American football quarterback*

"The soul is placed in the body like a
rough diamond, and must be
polished, or the luster of it will never
appear."
> *- Daniel Defoe*
> *English writer*

"I really think that American gentlemen are the better after all, because kissing your hand may make you feel very good but a diamond and a sapphire bracelet lasts forever."
- Anita Loos
American screenwriter

"There comes a moment when the silence between two people can have the purity of a diamond."
- Philippe Dijian, Betty Blue
Dijian (author) French film: Betty Blue

"There are two kinds of diamonds in this world: The diamond itself and the eyes full of love!"
- Mehmet Murat ildan
Turkish playwright

"I have always felt a gift diamond shines so much better than one you buy for yourself."
- Mae West
American actress

"True friends are like diamonds - bright, beautiful, valuable, and always in style."
- Nicole Richie
American actress

"Many individuals have, like uncut diamonds, shining qualities beneath a rough exterior."
- Juvenal
Roman poet

"I never hated a man enough to give him diamonds back."
- Zsa Zsa Gabor
Hungarian-American actress

"The diamond is the hardest stone - to get."
- Evan Esar
American humorist

"Diamonds are a girl's best friend and a man's worst enemy."
- Anonymous

"Diamonds are forever."

- Ian Fleming
English author

"A diamond is a chunk of coal that did well under pressure."
- Henry Kissinger
American political scientist

"True friends are like diamonds - bright, beautiful, valuable, and always in style."

- Nicole Richie
American actress

"Women not only love diamonds but are also strong like them."
- Anonymous

"Rough diamonds may sometimes be mistaken for worthless pebbles."

- Thomas Brown
Scottist philosopher and Poet

"I'm fascinated by diamonds. When I put diamonds on, my hands start to shake."

- Debra Messing
American actress

"I don't exercise. If God had wanted me to bend over, he would have put diamonds on the floor."

- Joan Rivers
American comedian

"Whenever I fail as a father or husband... a toy and a diamond always work."

- Shah Rukh Khan
Indian film actor, producer

Diamonds Timeline

The oldest diamonds formed under extreme pressure about 3 billion years ago, at depths between 90 and 120 miles, and temperatures of 1652-2372.

About 900 million years ago many of the youngest diamonds are formed.

At about 3000 BC, a diamond was set in the middle of the *ankh* (the Egyptian symbol for life). Egyptians believed that diamonds symbolized courage, truth, and power - and that they also represented the sun.

Around 2500 BC, the Chinese use diamonds to cut stones as part of the tool-making process.

In the fourth century BC, diamonds are mined in India and traded as adornments between India And China. The *Arthashastra* (Indian treatise from the second and third century BC) mentions the diamond trade in India. In addition to being used to adorn people (on rings), diamonds are also used to represent the eyes of the statues of deities.

Alexander the Great

In 327 BC, the great conqueror, Alexander the Great (King of the Greek state of Macedonia) brings diamonds from India to Europe.

296 BC The "Arthasastra", a Sanskrit manuscript, mentions diamonds.

A Chinese work from the third century BC mentions that diamonds were worn by foreigners to ward off evil. The Chinese, however, initially use diamonds as a "jade cutting knife."

The Roman writer, Pliny the Elder (AD 23-79), mentions "*adamas*" ("unconquerable") for their ornamental and engraving uses.

In 500 ACE, the *"Ratnapariska"* is written in India. It contains all of India's knowledge of diamonds.

In 1074, diamonds are used as jewelry to decorate the crown of a Hungarian queen.

The first major diamond cutting industry begins in Venice, Italy.

Didier Descouens

The city soon becomes the diamond trading capital of the world.

In 1375 the first guild of diamond cutters is formed in Nurnberg, Germany.

In the early 1400s, diamonds start being cut in Paris.

In 1458, Lodewyk van Berquem of Belgium created cut diamonds by using diamond dust to cut them.

In 1477 diamonds are first used in an engagement ring of Mary of Burgundy, now part of France.

It is gifted to her by the Archduke Maximillian of Austria.

This started the diamond engagement ring tradition.

In 1700, diamonds are discovered in Borneo.

In 1725, diamonds are discovered in Brazil (South America). Between 1730 and 1870, Brazil becomes the largest producer of diamonds.

1837 Charles Lewis Tiffany starts the Tiffany Diamond Company.

In the 1840s, diamonds are discovered in North America.

The "Eureka Diamond" is discovered in 1866 in South Africa, on the banks of the Orange River.

In 1869 another large diamond is found in South Africa on land owned by the De Beers brothers. After much energetic mining, the level of the land in the area lowered - and a deep open-pit mine is created, "the Kimberley Mine". The De Beers company acquires an alleged monopoly over world diamonds until 2005, when an antitrust lawsuit against De Beers is settled.

In the 1900s, diamond saws and jewelry lathes are developed.

In 1931, the GIA (Gemological Institute of America), is founded.

In 1947, the "A Diamond Is Forever" phrase is coined by DeBeers.

In the 1950s, the "Four C's diamond grading system" is introduced by the GIA (Gemological Institute of America).

1969 The Taylor-Burton diamond is purchased by the famous couple.

A major diamond mine, the Ekati, opens in Canada.

In 2014, Russia is the largest producer of diamonds in both value and volume.

Notes